Hello Westridge Readers!

Have MANY adventures aboard YOUR Train of Thought!

- Mister Lemur!

# Train of Thought

TRAIN OF THOUGHT
Copyright 2011
Hans Hartvickson
Printed in the United States of America
Second Edition

Published by
Ringtail Learning
San Francisco, CA

ISBN 13: 978-0-9828866-0-1

Library of Congress Control Number: 2010913806

For order information visit www.misterlemur.com.

This book is available at a quantity discount with bulk purchase for educational use. For information, please e-mail misterlemur@misterlemur.com and supply the title of the book, quantity, how the book will be used, and date needed.

Mister Lemur is a trademark of Hans Hartvickson.
Moving Children Forward, Taking Parents Back is a trademark of Hans Hartvickson.

Cover artwork by Kimberly Schwede.

A portion of profits from this book will be donated to charities supporting the protection of lemurs and/or lemur habitat.

Manufactured by Thomson-Shore, Dexter, MI (USA); RMA572TB589, March 2011

# DAILY DEPARTURES

# DAILY DEPARTURES

 This caboose indicates that you have reached the end of a story and it is time for your next departure. Bon Voyage!

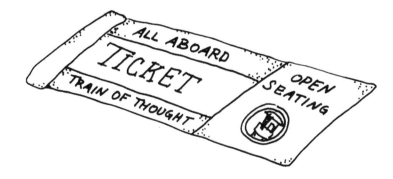

# TRAIN OF THOUGHT

Come and ride the train of thought,
it doesn't matter where.
To ride you simply close your eyes
or pick a spot and stare.

Sometimes you'll be the engineer,
sometimes you're on the ride,
and on this train you'll be amazed
at whom you'll sit beside.

You'll sit with former presidents,
you'll fly with astronauts,
you'll venture with magicians
as you travel through your thoughts.

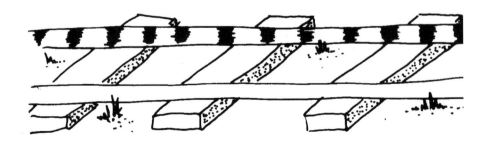

You'll wander in the mountains,
and you'll daydream by the shore,
and often when you board the train,
you won't know what's in store.

Stop to read good writers
who are witty and are fun,
'cause that's the kind of fuel
on which your train of thought will run.

And if traveling makes you tired
your sleeping car includes a bed,
and your train sets off to dream land,
for more adventures in your head.

# BAD BEAN DEFECT

After snacking on beans,
I began to suspect
that these beans contained
some kind of bad bean defect.

My stomach expanded,
my eyes got quite wide.
It felt like a hot spring
was gurgling inside

my belly, my gut,
or whatever you'd call it;
it's about to explode
and I'd like to forestall it!

This pain is not normal,
and please understand,
it feels like I've swallowed
a whole marching band.

They're playing four trumpets,
two horns, a trombone
and the band leader's shouting
through his megaphone.

They marched past my kidney
to my large intestine,
if you know how to silence them,
yell the suggestion!

My mom called the doc
who said, "Give him some Tums.
That should help silence
the horns and the drums."

And the doctor was right,
and the band went on break
and my stomach returned
to just a dull ache.

So surely by now
you must know what this means;
next time I am hungry...
I won't eat three cans of beans!

# SUMMER VACATIONS

I'm tired of the winter time.
I'd like to go away.
I'd hop a flight to summer time
if I could find a way.

I thought this was impossible,
that was, you see, until
I met a man from São Paulo,
a city in Brazil.

He talked about the Amazon,
and Ipanema Beach.
He said that he spoke Portuguese
and had come here to teach.

He then said, "South America's
not in this hemisphere,
so we're enjoying summer time
when it is winter here."

"When you are living with short days,
our days are very long.
When you enjoy the summer breeze,
our winter wind is strong."

"When you dream of white Christmas days
we're out on summer break.
When we ski on a mountain top
you're skiing on a lake."

That didn't make much sense to me,
but as I would learn later,
seasons come at different times
down south of the equator.

So I learned that by splitting time
between each hemisphere,
I can have two summer times
in each and every year.

This bit of science that I learned
has wondrous applications.
'Cause if I have two summers,
I'll have two summer vacations!

## PETTING ZOO

An advertisement caught my eye
tacked to a pole as I walked by.
And though the writing was quite bad,
I had to stop and read this ad.

The writing looked like chicken scratch.
The colored thumb tacks did not match.
The message was not all that clear,
but I will reproduce it here:

"My name is Earl, allow me to
invite you to our petting zoo,
where you'll meet ponies, pigs and sheep,
and things that slither, crawl and creep."

"Some pigmy goats and jumping frogs,
and several kinds of dingo dogs,
a flying squirrel, a porcupine,
some species that are in decline."

"A seal pup, a baby ox,
a cockatiel that never talks,
a rabbit with two lucky feet
and one outspoken parakeet."

"At night we have a flock of bats,
two raccoons and feral cats.
To meet them all and many more
just come and knock on Earl's door."

---

Dingo dog: Australian wild dog.
Feral cat: Cat that has to take care of itself without the help of people.

It seemed like something fun and new
so I said, "I will see this zoo"
and since it was a summer day
I thought, "I'll bike there straight away."

As soon as they saw me arrive,
the animals all came alive
with squeaks and yips and yelps and chirps
and grunts and clucks and chips and burps.

I could not think above the sound.
The rowdy flock all gathered round.
While some just seemed to run about,
others seemed to check me out.

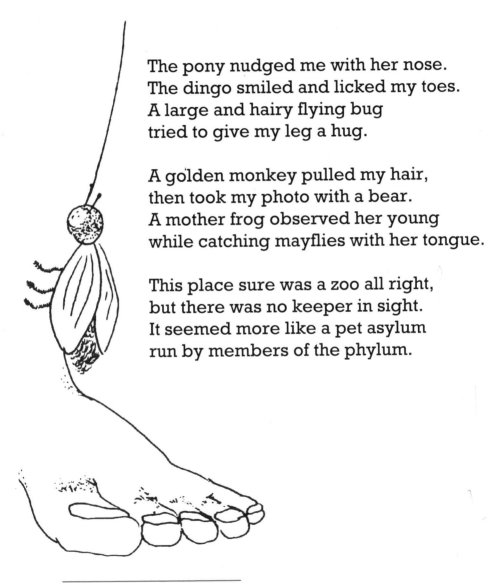

The pony nudged me with her nose.
The dingo smiled and licked my toes.
A large and hairy flying bug
tried to give my leg a hug.

A golden monkey pulled my hair,
then took my photo with a bear.
A mother frog observed her young
while catching mayflies with her tongue.

This place sure was a zoo all right,
but there was no keeper in sight.
It seemed more like a pet asylum
run by members of the phylum.

Asylum: A safe place; a refuge.
Phylum: A classification of organisms based on a general body type.

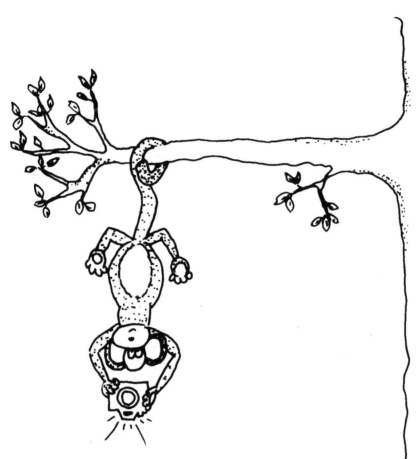

An old grey owl, wise and large,
appeared to be the one in charge,
and so I said, "I'm quite surprised
at how this zoo is organized."

"Though your collection is impressive,
they're hard to pet and they're aggressive."

The owl slowly cocked his head,
in thought, before he finally said,

"My boy, at this here petting zoo
the animals come to pet you.
The cats and bats and rats at Earl's
have come to pet the boys and girls."

"So stand there grinning ear to ear;
don't move too fast when they come near.
I hope that I have read you right.
You do not seem like you would bite."

So I said, "Fine, I will be pet."
But what I learned I won't forget.
How much you like a petting zoo
depends upon your point of view!

## DEN HEAD

The waking bear, large and confused,
still groggy from the months he snoozed,
begins to wake up with a yawn,
and notices that winter's gone.

He rubs his paws over his eyes.
His droopy lids pop in surprise.
'Cause in the mirror, standing there...
a bear with gnarley den head hair!

It looks as though, during the night,
two hair stylists had had a fight
and made a "bear do" most extreme,
with curlers, gel and styling cream.

He's got a faux-hawk on one side,
the other's poofy and blow-dried.
His back is spiked from head to toe,
his tail's knotted in a bow.

Eventually he'll fish and swim
and his hair will not stick to him.
Then through the summer and the fall
the bear won't have den head at all.

But as the fall is winding down,
and snowflakes start to dust the ground,
he'll climb back in his winter den
to start his hair cycle again.

And just how he'll emerge next spring
depends on what the winter'll bring.
The forecast is for heavy snow,
so I forecast a Grizzly Fro!

# TOUCAN

I'm not sure when he first appeared
but there's a Toucan in my beard.
Now every time I try to speak,
he pokes my chin with his curved beak.

He pokes my chin as if to say,
"Throw a little bread my way.
Throw me just a little piece
and all the poking will decrease."

As strange as this is going to sound,
I like having this bird around.
He keeps my beard clear of debris,
and I, for him, am like a tree.

It's not what I'd sought to arrange.
My friends and neighbors think it's strange.
But this is more than just exotic.
I would call it "symbiotic."

Symbiotic: Plants and/or animals living together for a better life.

## EYEBALL

In Transylvania
where Dracula dwells,
kids play different games
'tween the recess bells.

They play football, basketball
and baseball like most,
but their favorite game
puts the "gross" in engrossed.

Yes the Ghoul's School kids'
favorite pastime of all
is a keep away game
that is known as "Eye Ball."

Daily recess time starts
when a troll rings a gong
and the school speakers blare
out the "Thriller" theme song.

Then the freaks and the ghouls
all pour out from the class
and race out to the field,
a rectangle of grass,

where a monstrous kid
who looks quite appalling,
will let out a howl
to start the Eye Balling.

On the cue of that sound
they will all run about,
trying to knock
someone's eyeball right out!

They'll swing wings or claws
or they'll flail a tail,
at some other ghoul,
trying to make an eye sail

from that monster's head
to the field of play,
so someone can grab it
and play keep away.

When the gong rings again
and recess finally ends,
they'll put back their eyes
and they'll all remain friends,

though some end with more
and some end with less,
and some go back to class
in a big bloody mess!

By the time he leaves school,
if a monster is great,
though he started with two eyes,
he'll end up with eight.

So if you ever notice
a Cyclops about,
now you'll know he played Eye Ball
and one eye was knocked out!

---

Cyclops (plural Cyclopes): One-eyed giants from Greek mythology.

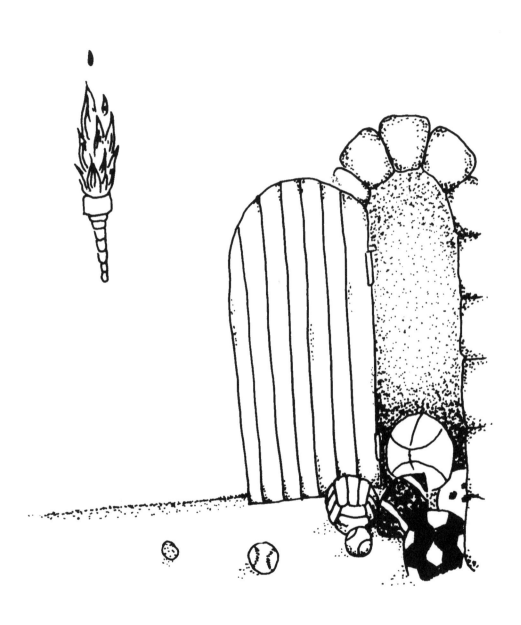

20

## TIMING

To get an arrow in a bull's eye
I have always found it,
easiest to shoot the arrow first,
...then paint the target around it.

# ANNIE'S SMILE

Annie dropped her smile
while she was running for the bus.

She thought that someone stole it
and she thought that it was us.

She thought that someone took it
'cause they wanted her to worry.

I think Annie lost her smile
'cause she is always in a hurry.

# KANGAROO CRUTCHES

Bounding through the vast outback
a kangaroo felt his knee crack.
He landed funny on a hop,
his twisted knee went "crackle-pop."

A joey with an injured knee
does not have much mobility.
They put a brace on nice and tight
and gave him heaps of Vegemite.

The doctor said he could not hop
'til all the pain and swelling stop.
But if he could not hop or bound,
how could this joey get around?

So what exactly do you do
to help an injured kangaroo?
The Aussies found a jolly trick…
they put him on a pogo stick!

Now he can bound with other 'roos
and getting hurt's not such bad news.

---

Outback: A hot, dry part of Australia where very few people live.
Joey: A young kangaroo.

23

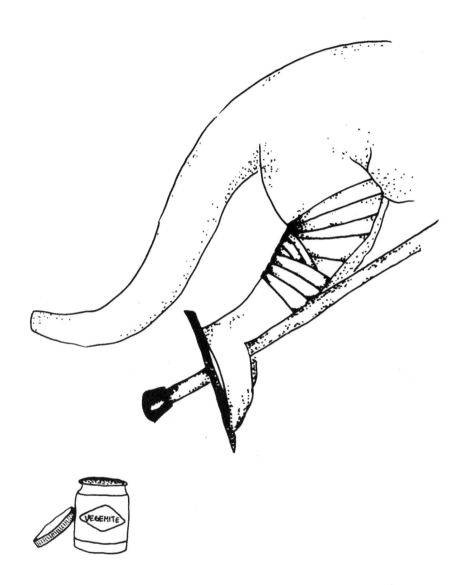

# GENERAL JACK

Young Judy hated clean up duty.
The playroom was a mess.
So nicks and nacks and jacks and tacks
would always coalesce

around the places people walk
and General Jack, her dad,
preferred that things be neat and tight.
Her messes made him mad.

Coalesce: To join into a single group.

The General was a high strung man,
he never stood in place.
Whenever he would think and scheme
he'd fidget and he'd pace.

He'd pace around the yard and house
with purpose in his gaze,
then pace back to his war room
with his maps and his displays.

Young Judy knew at times like these
to stay out of his way.
She'd sneak off to her playroom
to make crafts or simply play.

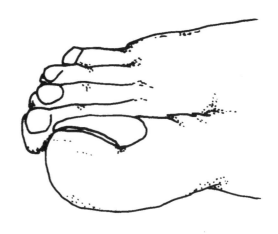

Well, one such day she dropped a tack
along the playroom floor,
but Judy didn't pick it up
'cause cleaning was a chore.

She thought, "I'll do it later"
but that thought soon slipped her mind.
It didn't seem that Judy
was domestically inclined.

Soon General Jack was on the phone
with Hard of Hearing Harry,
the oldest Sergeant Major
in the U.S. military.

And as they talked about the plans
for soldiers in Iraq,
the General paced around the room...
until he found that tack.

When his bare foot came stomping down,
he hollered his objection,
and Hard of Hearing Harry
thought there'd been an insurrection.

---

Domestically inclined: Describes one who enjoys or is interested in housekeeping.
Insurrection: A rising up against established authority; rebellion.

"General Sir, are you ok?
You just let out a yell..."
The General said, "It was a tack"
but Harry'd not heard well.

So Harry said, "Please say again –
I missed what you had said."
"I said, 'I just stepped on a tack.'"
The General's face burned red.

Still Harry said, "You stepped on what?
I don't hear well, of course."
The General yelled, "A tack! A tack!"
with emphasis and force.

So Hard of Hearing Harry
dropped the line and called all fronts.
He ordered a surprise attack,
and said, "Begin at once!"

Before he knew what happened
it was too late to turn back,
and no one was caught more surprised
than four star General Jack.

The moral of the story
is "It's best to do your chores"
...unless of course you're into
accidently starting wars.

## TEPIN PEPPER

*"The World's Hottest Pepper"*

You have not lived until you've tried
a Tepin pepper deep fat fried.
My first bite made me squirm and choke.
My ears emitted greenish smoke.

My eyes got wide, my face turned red.
I yelled for water, milk and bread.
If one were handy, heaven knows,
I would have sucked a garden hose.

And finally I did stop the blaze...
by gargling with some mayonnaise!

But so my friends would be impressed
I said, "It's great!" ...and ate the rest.

# ROTISSERIE ME

I toss and turn and turn and toss, my night of sleep's a total loss. I think I had too much caffeine, I'm buzzing like a slot machine. First I got cold then I got hot, I rolled my covers in a knot. I doubt I caught a single "z", I slept like a rotisserie. With all this turning side to side, I look like I've been mummified. My sheets are wrapped into a shroud that would make Tutankhamen proud. But since I've no place else to write, I guess its time to say good niizzzzzz...

# CONTINENTAL PLATES

We're tired of leaving hungry
from the Thirsty Bear Café,
so we've planned to start a restaurant
where it's done a different way:

a place with massive meals
to meet the biggest appetites,
a place with giant forks
where people feast on giant bites,

a place with salads big as fields,
and county-sized entrees,
that a normal man could barely eat
if he had three full days,

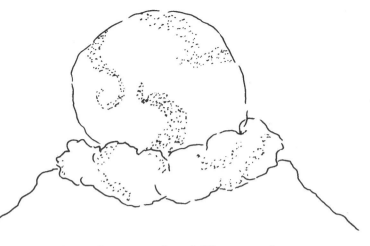

a place with glasses sized like pools
and soup bowls sized like lakes.
We'll have our own construction team
to build our high-rise cakes.

But how can we serve meals this big?
We've had several debates.
It seems that we must serve our meals
on continental plates.

But when we tried to dig them up,
(imagine what this takes!)
we found that simply moving them
created huge earthquakes.

So instead we'll start an ice cream shop,
one that will never close.
And we'll serve tons of ice cream
in the cones of volcanoes.

Though doing that might make a mess,
and cause a slight disruption,
just think how happy we'll all be
next time there's an eruption!

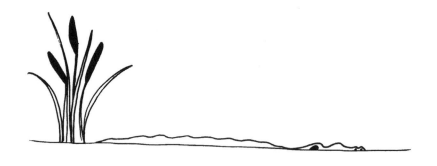

## THAT'S A CROC

If you stomp around a swamp
it's best to know your facts
on how to ward off gators, snakes
and crocodile attacks.

Crocs look much like gators
but a real swamper knows,
while gators have a wide brimmed snout
crocs have a pointy nose.

But if you see a bumpy back
don't stop to check the breed.
You'd better head for dryer ground
or you'll be Crocagator feed!

# COME AND JOIN THE BODY BAND

Come and join the body band
we're making up a song.
Unless you've got no body
this is how you play along.

Hiccup through a poster tube,
cough low to add some bass.
Buzz like you're a bumblebee
while you contort your face.

Breathe like you've just run a mile,
snore like a lumber jack.
Howl as though you are a wolf
that just stepped on a tack.

Make a drum beat on your thighs,
"tick-tock" like you're a clock.
In this symphony we all can be
Johann Sebastian Bach.

Pull a finger, pop a cheek,
click your heels in time.
Take that quarter in your shorts
and rub it 'gainst  a dime.

You say you have no instrument?
I don't think you understand.
'Cause if you've got a body
you are in the body band!

## THE WRITERS' BLOCK

There are lots of blocks in any town,
of homes and shops and stores.
Did you know there's a writers' block,
in my town, and in yours?

You may not recognize this block,
most maps don't point it out.
But when you're in a writers' block,
you'll know without a doubt.

Your way with words will wander,
the right phrases won't be found.
You may as well put down your pen,
get up and walk around.

Some folks walk the writers' block,
in search of Neverland.
Some seek Shakespeare in his yard
with fountain pen in hand.

Some find The Wolf and Riding Hood
engaging in a truce.
Some see Harry Potter hang out
with The Grinch from Dr. Seuss.

Great biographers, sportswriters,
Charles Schultz and Charlie Brown,
have all spent time in the writers' block
that is within their town.

So when your creative writing
ends up stuck behind a rock,
just know you've got great company,
residing on your block.

And know that you'll soon move along,
as all the others do.
You are only here to visit.
You are only passing through.

## MOUSE GUEST

My neighbor has the strangest mouse
that you have ever seen.
He soaps his paws before he eats,
and keeps his mouse nest clean.

He is so clean that he won't drink
the water from the toilet,
until he puts it in a pan
to sanitize and boil it.

Last time I went to visit
and I walked into the room,
the mouse was in the corner
with a dustpan and a broom.

I've seen him run the base boards
with a rag removing dust.
He gets no health insurance
and he'll work for crumbs and crust.

Because he's such a good mouse guest
this mouse is free to roam.
My parents want a mouse like that
to dust and mop our home!

Instead we have a twelve pound mouse
that chased our cat away,
a mouse who thinks our kitchen is
his personal buffet.

He'll raid the freezer late at night,
and then not close the door.
Each time he steals cereal
he trails it on the floor.

Nothing 'gainst my neighbor's mouse,
but if pressed I'll confess
that I'd rather have my messy mouse
to blame for every mess!

## DOG CATCHER

Only eight kids showed up for the baseball game
and a baseball team should have nine,
so we decided that somebody's dog better play,
and the team selected mine.

Catching Frisbees in his teeth
is Henry's main forte,
but since he really has no arm
where should we have him play?

He's a little short to play first base
and so our intuition
was to have him wear the catcher's gear
and play in that position.

The debate became an easy one
as soon as someone saw
that Johnny had a catcher's mitt
that fit on Henry's paw.

But Henry didn't want a mitt,
and that's common for a hound.
He'd catch the pitches in his mouth
then run back to the mound.

Now, throwing a slobber covered ball
takes a special kind of skill,
but our pitcher pitched on well enough,
that was, of course, until,

old Henry got distracted
in the middle of the third.
He dropped the ball and sprinted off
to chase a wounded bird.

And though we did get Henry back
after some delay,
he'd lost his focus in the chase,
and didn't want to play.

He chewed the shortstop's shoelaces,
dug a hole behind third base;
he missed a sign for hit and run
and licked the umpire's face.

He wasn't handy with a bat
though he did lay down a bunt,
but what happened in the 9th
was the game's defining stunt.

The other team's best player
was a boy named Wade DeBritt,
who lead off the 9th inning
with an infield base hit.

We were leading four to three,
the game was close and tight.
We couldn't go to extras,
we were running out of light.

The next two batters grounded out.
DeBritt moved to third base.
Of all the times to drop the ball,
this was not the place.

But sure enough old Henry
couldn't block a wild pitch.
The ball kicked off the backstop
and into a drainage ditch.

DeBritt started home from third
to tie the game at four.
The ball had skipped so far away
we all thought he would score.

But Henry's a retriever,
he can really shake a leg.
He got the ball and blocked the plate,
and he applied the tag!

Then they made this odd notation
in the scorer's scorebook log:
DeBritt was tagged out stealing
by the second baseman's dog.

## SPELLING TEST

It hardly strkies me as worhtwhile,
to invset time leraning spelling.
Wriitng thnigs down semes ineffciient
compraed to simply telling

Soemone exatcly what to do,
in person or on the phoen
And I've heard theer are no seplling tests at all
when you are grown.

So I'm not gonig to stduy spelling,
I don't think it's improtant for me,
Besieds, I spell pretty well rihgt now,
woudln't you agere?

## PECULIAR

Some might say I'm peculiar,
others would just say "unique."
In most ways I look like a normal young boy,
'cept my nose was replaced with a beak.

I'd have gladly traded my arms for wings,
and having gills would be pretty neat.
I could swim as fast as a dolphin,
if I had flippers instead of my feet.

But now people say I pick at my food,
and my glasses will not stay in place.
It's hard to put on a turtleneck shirt.
My teacher says, "Why the long face?"

I popped a balloon that my grandma gave me.
It scared me, I let out a "skwak!"
My parents put me in speech therapy
because I chirp whenever I talk.

No one seems willing to kiss me.
I love looking for fish in the stream.
I find that I'm strangely attracted to worms.
Oh – good morning – that was only a dream?

# COUNT EASE

Have you tried to count the counties
on a map of the U.S.?

Today I tried to count them all
so that I could impress
my uncle who is making maps -
I wanted him to see
that I was quite an expert
on U.S. geography.

And just to make it clear to him
my knowledge is complete,
I made a plan to memorize
each county's county seat.

A

ABBELVILLE
ACADIA
ACCOMACK
ADA
ADAIR
ADAMS
ADDISON
AIKEN
AITKIN
ALACHUA
ALAMANCE
ALAMEDA
ALAMOSA
ALBANY
ALBEMARLE
ALCONA
ALCORN
ALUETIANS EAST BOROGH
ALUETIANS WEST CENSUS BAREW
ALEXANDRIA
ALFALFA
ALGER
ALLAMAKEE
ALLEGANY
ALLEGHANY
AILEN
MLEGHENI
ALPENA
ALPINE
AMADOR
AMELIA
AMHERST
AMITE
ALMODYA DIER LONIS
ANCHORAGE BOROGH
ABERSON
ANDREV
ANDREWS
ANDROSCOGN
ANGLINA
MME ARUNDEL
ANOKA
ANSON

County seat: A town or city that is the center of county government.

I started counting counties
and I counted through the A's.
I counted up one hundred twelve.
This could go on for days!

I counted on. It got worse...
two hundred eighteen B's.
I think next time I'll count the states,
or just the seven seas.

And if you'd like to stump your friends
next time you're feeling sporty,
the count of counties in the U.S. is...

three thousand one hundred forty!

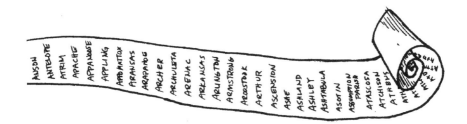

## COWABUNGA

My uncle Howard always makes
the most amazing farm fresh shakes.
But what I didn't know 'til now
is that they come straight from a cow.

He drives a milk cow up a ridge,
up to the Cowabunga Bridge.
Then carefully, so he's not gored
he will attach a bungee cord
between her legs, around her waist,
ensuring it is tightly placed.

Then he'll yell "Yaa!" and crack the whip,
which gives her such a start she'll slip.
She'll fall then spring and spring and bounce,
the milk will shake, every last ounce.

And then, he says, "I milk her quick,
before she can get motion sick."

And if the bungee cord should break?

"We'll get no milk... but we'll have steak."

49

50

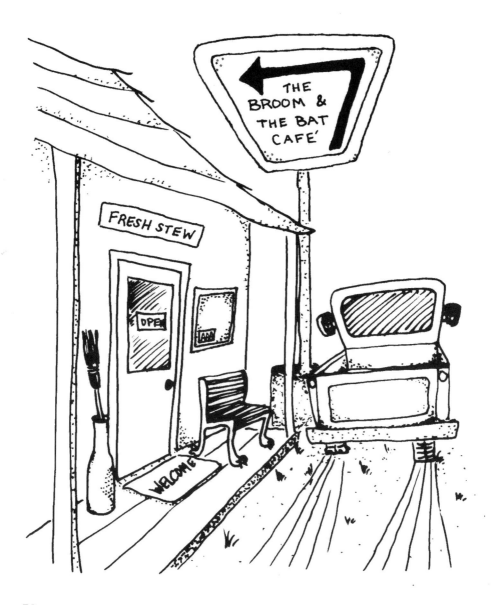

51

## THE SALEM SANDWICH
## TRIBULATIONS

Driving through Salem
my tire went flat
by a little café
called The Broom and the Bat.

The café window shown
a AAA sign,
so I wandered inside
to get help and to dine.

I was hungry from driving
and needed to eat.
Since the restaurant was empty
I picked a good seat.

---

Salem Witch Trials: Trials in and near Salem, Massachusetts in the year
1692 where women were accused of being witches.
AAA: American Automobile Association.

The waitress looked me over
and said, "What do you want?
We're known for our stew
in this fine restaurant."

I said, "Thanks but no thanks."
She didn't hide her surprise
when I asked for the sandwich,
and, "Please hold the fries."

She said, "Very well sir,
if that is your wish.
What kind of sandwich?"

"I'll take the fish."

The décor was eclectic,
old cauldrons and pots
and pictures of full moons,
in various spots.

There was lots of commotion
from the restaurant's back room,
some gurgling, a cackle,
and then a loud "boom."

I read while I waited,
my nose in a book.
I lost track of time
and how long it took.

That sandwich took nearly
an hour to prepare.
When the waitress returned,
she looked worse for the wear.

I wish I had thought to ask,
"Why the delay?"
But I was so ravenous,
I bit in straight away.

Because I was starving,
I ate with much haste,
and I ate the first half
before I noticed the taste.

It was dry.
It was crusty.
It was bitter and sticky.
And I'm not a food snob.
I'm not even picky!

I stood up to complain
but no one could be found.
Then I heard a loud "woosh"
and I turned right around

to see half of my sandwich
was leaving the room,
flying astride
of the janitor's broom!

That shock was bad,
but what was much worse,
before the sandwich flew out,
she called out this curse,

"Double, double,
with a strawberry shake.
A sandwich in Salem?
You've made a mistake!

Next time you should order
granola and fruit.
Now I will turn you
into a newt!"

I yelled to the waitress,
"I'm not going to pay!
Half of my sandwich
has just flown away!"

"If you don't pay your bill sir
you're going to jail,
and I can't help but notice...
you're growing a tail!"

So next time I'm in Salem,
I'll only eat fruit,
'cause that ornery old sandwich
turned me into a newt.

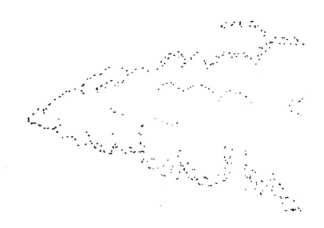

## THAT'S COOL

It was so hot last night I felt
as though my head would surely melt.
Which made me think, "It would be nice
to have a home built out of ice."

I guess I must have thought out loud,
'cause suddenly there was a cloud
of orangish glowing eerie smoke
...and then a magic genie spoke.

"Your home will be as you have chosen,
made of ice, completely frozen."

When those thirteen words were said,
then instantly I felt my bed,
and the ceilings and the floors,
the chairs, the lights, the roof, the doors,

the windows, sinks  and storage chest,
the couch, TV and all the rest
become completely made of ice.
And wow did that cool air feel nice!

It was the coolest house I'd seen,
it felt just like an ice machine.
It felt amazing when I said it …
…but then I started to regret it.

'Cause then I hollered, "I forgot
to wish the air outside less hot."
And suddenly I heard and felt
the walls and ceiling start to melt!

The genie with the orange-ish glow
said, "So long now, I have to go.
You're welcome for your house of ice,
but let me give you some advice."

Next time ask for a cool breeze,
perhaps a drop of ten degrees,
but when you ask sir, I implore,
be careful what you're asking for!

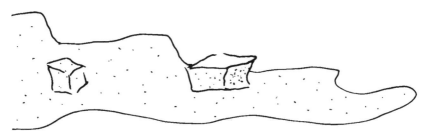

## DUCK DENTISTRY

My name is Dennis and I'm a dentist,
I only work on ducks.
I used to work on gophers,
rabbits, beavers and woodchucks.

There aren't many others like me,
duck dental care's a brand new art.
There's not much to do to help ducks chew,
...so how'd I get my start?

As you may know, ducks don't have teeth,
they smoosh things with their bill.
So ducks did not need dentistry,
that was, of course, until

there came cosmetic dentistry,
to help enhance their smile,
and ducks are dapper looking birds,
that like to be in style.

Some ducks demanded big false teeth,
and sparkly ducky smiles,
and asked that they be light in weight,
because ducks fly for miles.

Then I invented duck veneers,
big ducky pearly whites,
with alloy made by scientists
for NASA's deep space flights.

With that I launched duck dentistry,
a whole new health care field.
I'm making all the flashy things
for which the ducks appealed.

So next time you see a mallard
and that mallard smiles at you,
toss her a snack, quack right back,
and show your smile too.

Veneer: A thin layer of material placed over a tooth surface.

## TWO THOUSAND FORTY-THREE

What do you think you will be
when it's two thousand forty-three?

If I were asked to make a bet,
I'd say it's not invented yet,
that you'll do something not yet known,
like fix a "Woosh" or fly a "Kone."

Perhaps you'll cure a new disease,
or sail a new-found planet's seas
aboard a ship that floats on air
while sitting in the captain's chair.

You have no plan? No need to fret,
your job's not been invented yet!

## HAT DANCE

I highly suggest, if you should get the chance,
stay up Saturday night, and go to the hat dance.
If you never do see it, your life's incomplete.
It's the one time per week the hats show their feet.

Yes Saturday night, when everyone is asleep,
they come from their closets, or where people keep
their bowlers, sombreros and pinwheel caps,
their ski hats, their free hats with fuzzy ear flaps,
their cowboy hats, helmets and yarmulkes too,
hats that are green, red white yellow and blue.

And they go into town, to the great hat dance hall,
and the hats have a party, a regular ball!
They hit the floor dancing, expressing their whims,
bobbing their crowns and shaking their brims.

They dance through the evening, dancing until,
they finally wear out and they settle their bill,
and head back to the rack, their version of bed,
to be ready by morning for somebody's head.

No it's not to be missed, if you do get the chance,
take a Saturday night, and go to the hat dance.

## MY RAIN SQUEEZE

The grass is brown, the lake is low.
The mountains didn't get much snow.
So help me end this summer drought.
Let's all grab clouds and squeeze 'um out.

## I'M ALL EARS

Well yes, I'm listening! I'm all ears.
That sounds less strange than it appears.

I've heard of warts from handling frogs,
and fleas and ticks from petting dogs,
but something no one had made clear,
is why you'd grow an extra ear.

Were it just one I'd not despair,
but then I grew an extra pair.
First two then four then six then eight.
Who knew new ears grew at this rate?

When there were ten I sat and cried,
but still my new ears multiplied,
'til soon they ran my width and height
and new ones grew in day and night.

In an attempt to find the cause,
I called up one of my in-laws,
a well-trained, local "E-N-T,"
and she explained it all to me:

"This ear growth is an adaptation
on kids without much concentration.
They grow, as far as I can tell,
on people who don't listen well."

So listen up or live in fear
that you may grow an extra ear!

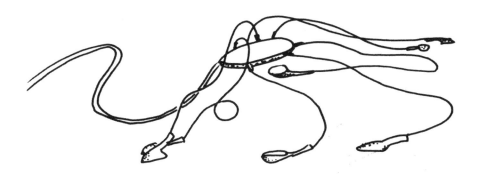

E-N-T: Doctor who specializes in ear, nose and throat care.

## THREEPLE

I'd like to live like an explorer,
and travel to never seen lands...
places where people speak only in threes,
with three fingers on each of their hands.

I'd travel someplace undiscovered,
someplace that is really remote,
someplace where you parachute to a small town,
then travel three days in a boat

to encounter a people nobody has seen,
in three villages tucked in the trees.
They shake your foot when they greet you.
Their words are said only in threes.

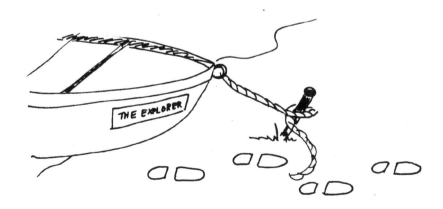

THE EXPLORER

They build huts from a weave of three grasses
that grow in three different locations.
All of their weekends are three full days long.
Every month they take three week vacations.

They awaken each morning three minutes past seven.
Each day they eat three three-course meals.
The national sport is the three-legged race.
Their bicycles all have three wheels.

They play lots of baseball,
where three strikes you're out,
with three bases and a home plate.

And they won't let you swim
for at least three full hours,
after the last three things you ate.

But after three weeks I will want to go home,
and leave the land of Threeple.
'Cause all of the Threeple seem strangely the same,
and I'd like to meet three new people.

## WILL CHEW FOR YOU

Ralph's an enterprising dog
who likes to earn his keep.
He works a pair of daytime jobs
while other dogs would sleep.

I certainly don't make him work,
in fact, I think it's strange,
each time Ralph packs his lunch and leaves
for odd jobs he'll arrange.

He hangs around two blocks from school
in shades and a trench coat,
and since Ralph can't speak English
he had someone write this note:

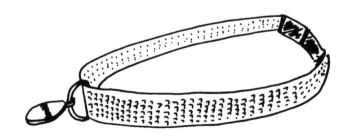

Enterprising: Demonstrating initiative, imagination and a willingness to
undertake new projects.

"Didn't get your homework done?
Don't worry you're in luck.
I'll make your problems disappear
for just one measly buck."

" I'll slobber on that paper
for as much time as it takes
'til your homework is unreadable...
and so are your mistakes!"

"I'll chew and shred and gnash and gnaw
for as long as you need,
to make sure what's not swallowed
is impossible to read."

"And then I'll do a leg lift,
to be sure my work's complete.
I'll pretend that it's on fire
and I'll water down each sheet."

"When I'm done with my business,
your poor teach will have no doubt
that she is not paid enough
to try to sort this out."

"So you'll get an extension
of at least one extra day.
To buy that kind of extra time
one buck's not too much to pay."

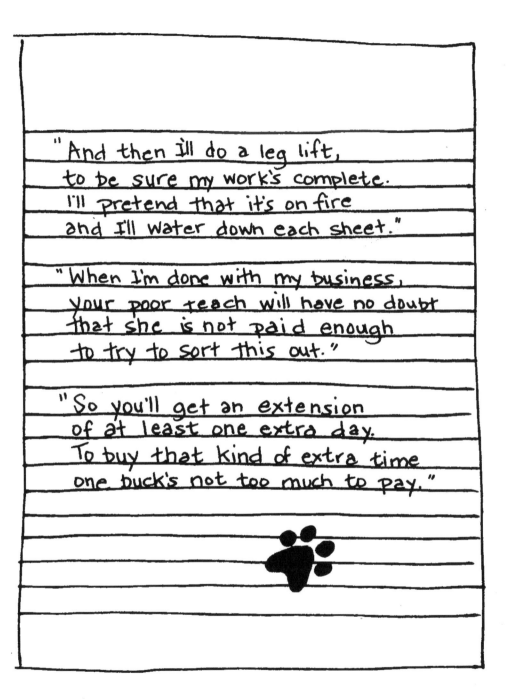

So that's my enterprising Ralph
who likes to earn his keep
by chewing up kids' homework
while most other dogs would sleep.

Ralph makes a lot of money
on his homework eating biz,
and I don't take a nickel
'cause the money is all his.

## CRAB POT

Am I the only one who feels
like I have been robbed by the seals?
See, every time I fish for crab
they see my bait and make a grab.
And every time they steal my bait
it makes me more and more irate.

These furry-faced aquatic bandits
really need to understand it's
not ok to take my bait,
even if it does taste great.

What's worse is they know how it feels
to have to fish for all your meals.
And yes, of course, I know they're cute,
but my mind is resolute.
So now atop my list of peeves
sit these little crab bait thieves.

## TALLER

I wish that I were tall enough
to ride the roller spin.
But though I stood tall as I could,
they would not let me in.

"You can read, now can't you son?
Your head must be this high."
But I could not quite reach that line,
no matter how I'd try.

The man said, "Maybe next year,
if you grow just like a weed."
He was not going to let me on,
though I did beg and plead.

So as my friends enjoyed the ride,
I stood aside to pout,
until a carnie whispered,
"I think I can help you out."

"There is a booth back in the back,
if you'll give them one dollar
they'll put you on a stretching rack
and stretch you 'til you're taller."

I looked at him, my eyes got big.
"This might be my chance!"
I started feeling round
in every pocket in my pants.

I added up the change I had.
I was short by a quarter.
I'd spent the rest of what I had
to place a hot dog order.

My carnie friend then spoke again,
"My boy you never know,
just tell them you're one quarter short,
but that you'd like to grow."

I told the booth attendant
that I was a little short,
but he just smiled and waived his hand,
"That's why we're here, old sport."

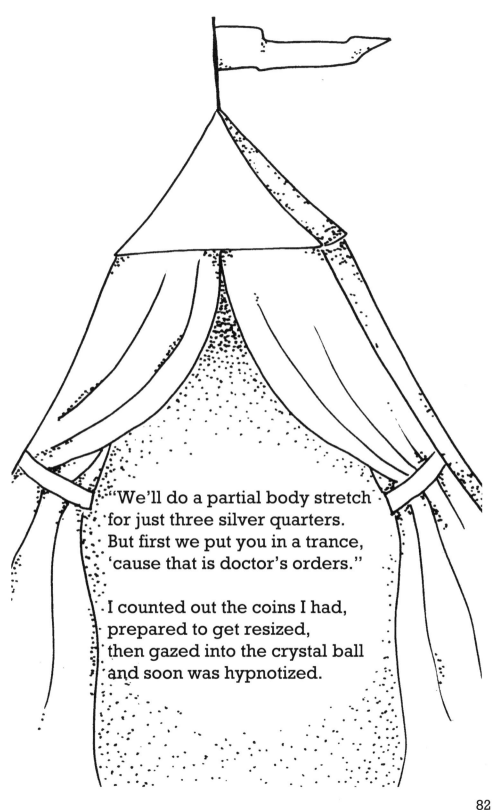

"We'll do a partial body stretch
for just three silver quarters.
But first we put you in a trance,
'cause that is doctor's orders."

I counted out the coins I had,
prepared to get resized,
then gazed into the crystal ball
and soon was hypnotized.

The next things I remembered
were familiar smells and sounds.
But everything looked different
as I surveyed my surrounds.

I looked above the crowd with ease
at all the tents and rides,
and I walked much more quickly
with my long and lanky strides.

I started getting funny looks,
and thought it was my height...
then someone with bad grammar said,
"His left don't match his right!"

So I looked down and what I saw
just froze me in my tracks.
One arm had not been stretched at all
while I was in the racks!

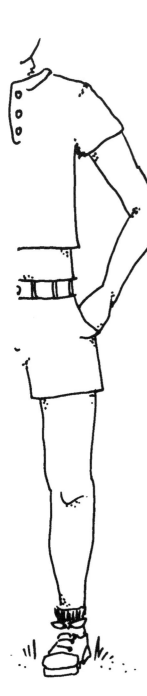

With that I strode off straightaway
back to the stretching station.
I found the rack attendant
and explained the situation.

"Just look at how my stretch turned out,
this whole thing has gone wrong.
My right arm has not changed at all.
My left is twice as long!"

He didn't stammer, break a sweat
nor'd he apologize.
Instead he simply smiled and said,
"This should be no surprise."

"You didn't have a dollar,
so I just assumed you knew...
when you gave us three quarters,
we stretched three quarters of you!"

## BRUCE THE MASSEUSE

Bruce the Masseuse opened a shop
and advertised so people would stop.
He wrote "Grand Opening" on his sign
and "Foot Massage $9.99."

Now customers were all he'd need,
but his first guest? A centipede!
That centipede took Bruce a week.
He was too tired to eat or speak.

Though that first week was quite horrific,
it taught Bruce to be specific.
So Bruce repainted his old sign
- the one that said "$9.99."

And in its place, here's what he put:
"Foot massage, five bucks per foot."

# MY UDDER BROTHER

I'm still not sure exactly how
I turned my brother into a cow.
The only thing of which I'm sure
is that I won't repeat this cure.

One Sunday evening, rather late,
his hiccupping would not abate.
He held his breath; he held his nose;
he held the crash position pose.
He sucked on bread; he chewed on ice;
but none of these cures would suffice.

Since nothing worked, I had no doubt
these hiccups needed driving out!
I was convinced he was possessed
by hiccup demons in his chest.

So I called up a friend of mine
who sells black magic stuff online,
like lucky charms and magic balls
and vitamins and voodoo dolls.

And he sent over cow hoof powder
which we mixed into a chowder,
a grayish goopy grisly slop,
they said would make his hiccups stop.

And since his case was quite advanced
I also read a chant and danced
an ancient native hiccup rite
...but something'd clearly not gone right.

Someday I'll find out what corrects
the first solution's side effects.
But when I do learn what to utter,
we won't have free milk and butter!

So to this day we're not sure how
I turned my brother into a cow.
My parents find the whole thing scary,
I just think its legend...dairy!

## THE BEE KEEPER

I believe I've been a bee keeper
for beyond three years now,
and I couldn't be more happy,
except my favorite word is "ow!"

If you look beneath the beech tree
you will see my hives of bees.
Every spring I'm flush with honeycomb
and healthy plants and trees.

People know me as the bee keeper.
They stay away and wave.
Most people think I'm crazy.
I think they're not very brave.

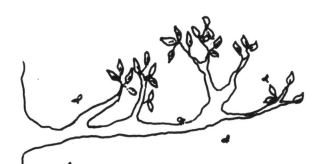

On April first, three years ago,
I donned my bee-keep suit,
and I ran throughout the startled town
along a crowded route.

I waived my hand and screamed and ran,
all through the town, then back,
yelling, "Killer bees are coming,
and they're going to attack!"

"You'll know them when they get here,
you can't miss the angry swarm.
They'll block the sun and fill the sky
more than the foulest storm!"

"We really don't have much time left,
but here are some details.
The ones that look like fighter jets
are usually the males."

"There is one way you might survive,
although your odds are slim.
These bees cannot stand water.
It's been shown that they can't swim."

They asked me for suggestions then,
and so, of course, I urged
they grab a tube to breathe through
and they spend the day submerged.

So everyone grabbed snorkel gear
and jumped in ponds or pools.
And they all stayed under water
'til I told them… "April Fools!!!"

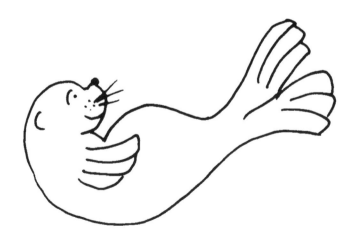

## OBSTACLE COURSE

The very first step in my obstacle course
requires you limbo beneath a small horse.
Then run 'round the track and jump over the hurdles
while holding a sting ray and two snapping turtles.

Do that with success and you're on to stage three,
where you will thumb wrestle a large chimpanzee.
But step number four may be toughest of all,
you must fence with a ferret while dribbling a ball.

I'm not really sure what you'd do in stage five.
No one has made it that far still alive!

## FLOSTA

In Foosa's lab she made a cross
between a pasta and a floss:
a fibrous food that you prepare
with left-overs from dental care.

First drop used Flosta in a pot
and stir it 'til it's soft and hot.
Then twirl it like your mom's spaghetti.
It turns green when it is ready.
Once it's cooked you simply toss
the Flosta with a three cheese sauce.

It's kinda gross but kinda neat.
It tastes like what you've had to eat.
And sure, it's kinda hard to chew,
but it's good for your teeth...and you!

So how's it taste? Well, it's alright,
though no one's had a second bite.
Taste testers gave us this report:
"Eat only as your last resort!"

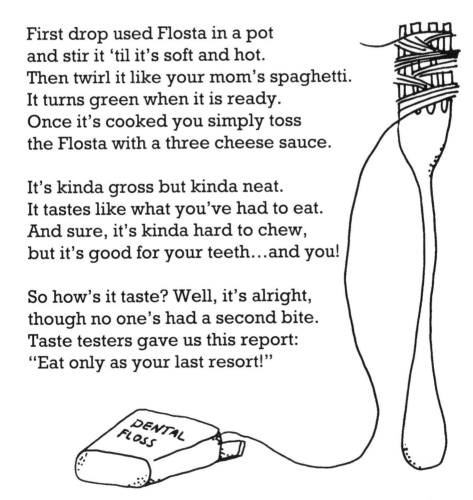

## WAITER

At the restaurant, I'm a waiter.
I asked to sit, but they said, "Later."
I said, "I'm starving, and dying of thirst!"
But they said, "Others were here first."

They said, "Just wait right over there.
We have a comfy waiting chair.
When there's a table we'll let you know.
Right now we're very busy though."

They asked if they could take my name,
(the only name to which I've claim),
but if they should take that from me,
they're taking my identity.

So I just smiled, "Not today,"
and they just shrugged and walked away.
Then I went to the waiting chair.
Two hours passed and I'm still there.

I guess they'll come and get me later,
but for now I'm still a waiter.
Since they serve what I really want,
I'm still a waiter at this restaurant.

96

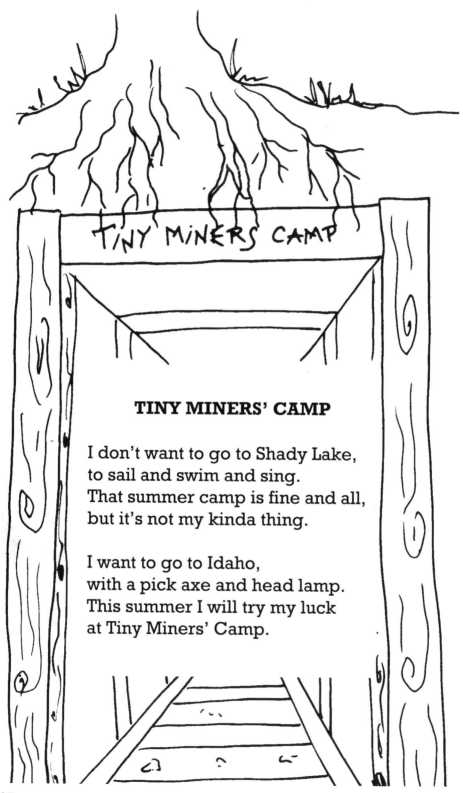

## TINY MINERS' CAMP

I don't want to go to Shady Lake,
to sail and swim and sing.
That summer camp is fine and all,
but it's not my kinda thing.

I want to go to Idaho,
with a pick axe and head lamp.
This summer I will try my luck
at Tiny Miners' Camp.

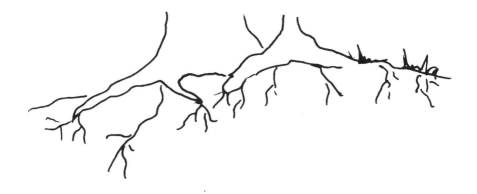

At sun-up we will pan for gold;
mid-day we mine for coal.
And I can keep the treasures
that I find down in the hole.

At night I'll sit by rock piles
hearing stories of brave men,
like Big John, who held the ceiling up
back when the mine caved in.

I'll sleep down in a mine shaft
in an old time miner's cot.
It'll feel like 1849
in a land that time forgot.

When friends try to impress me
with their summer arts and crafts,
I'll yawn and say, "That's nothing. Me?
I dug my own mine shafts!"

# MY NEW HAT

The hat I'd really like to have
has yet to be created.
It's not that no one's thought of it,
it's just quite complicated.

This hat has housing for a bird,
- a bright green cockatiel.
It's powered by two solar cells
and one electric eel.

Whenever I get hungry,
I'll just take it off my head.
Inside I'll find spaghetti
and a loaf of garlic bread.

My hat will have a camera,
a computer and a phone.
My hat will have some storage space
for everything I own.

But my hat won't be heavy,
I have engineered for that.
The other heads with hats to hold
will wish they held my hat!

And when my new hat's finished
everyone will stand in line...
now could someone please remind me
what I did with that design!

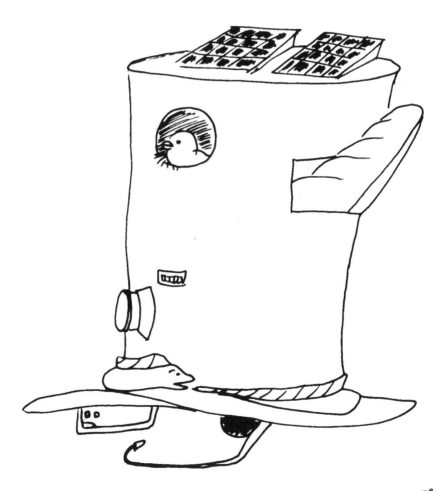

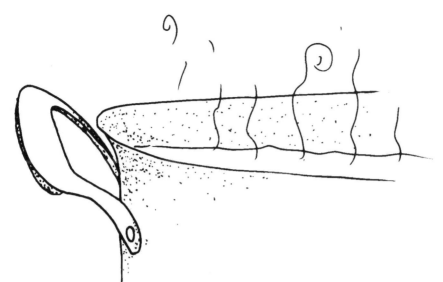

## CHOCOLATE FONDUE

Let's fill the biggest pot we've got
with melty cherry "choc-o-lat."
We'll add some flour and some spice
and heat it 'til it bubbles twice.

But fruit and berries are blasé.
Let's come at this a different way.
Then maybe we can write a book,
on new fondue that you can cook.

We'll put some sushi on long sticks,
and get our fishy chocolate fix.
We'll dip a stick of pinto beans
and angry bees (but not the queens),

Blasé: Uninteresting because of over-familiarity.

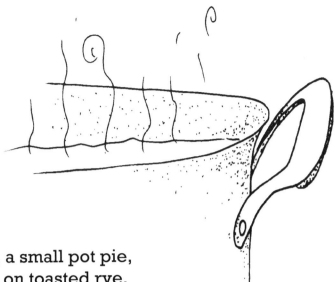

a deviled egg, a small pot pie,
a Cordon Bleu on toasted rye,
a kosher dill, a wedge of cheese,
some pork chow mien from overseas,

some mustard seed, a rack of lamb,
the contents of a can of Spam.
We'll tame a clove of garlic's wrath
by giving it a chocolate bath.

Now that we're done, upon inspection,
we may have gone the wrong direction.
I wonder if we ate too quick,
'cause suddenly I feel sick.

I think that we should think this through
before we publish on fondue.
Some things go well and some things won't.
I guess we'll call our book "Fon-Don't."

## SURPRISE PARTY

Surprise! It's a party!
Now you simply must have fun,
'cause you can't stop a party
once that party has begun.

You'd better lift your furrowed brow,
put twinkles in your eyes,
'cause you're the guest of honor.
What a great surprise!

Did you have something else to do?
Did you have something brewing?
This party will be much more fun,
than what you'd planned on doing!

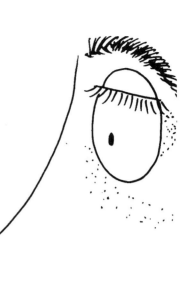

## LADYBUG

A ladybug landed on my nose.
I guess she's fine there, I suppose,
unless she needs a place to hide,
and she makes plans to come inside.

And while I'm willing to admit
there is some room where she could fit,
I think that she should think it through
before I have to…ah..AH-CHOO!

# CONNECT THE DOTS

Miss Foosa counted stars a lot
and thought, "I'll be an astronaut."
And though she could not quite say why,
she'd always loved the night-time sky.

She studied a celestial chart,
and learned to tell the stars apart.
She memorized the time of year
when each was in her hemisphere.

She'd lie some place that's nice and dark,
(a campsite or a quiet park)
connecting stars with made up lines
to find the Zodiac's twelve signs.

Virgo, Libra, Aquarius,
Cancer and Sagittarius,
Taurus, Gemini, Scorpio,
Aries, Pisces and Leo.

And, she noted, she was born
beneath the sign of Capricorn.

---

Celestial Chart: A chart or drawing that shows the relationship of
certain stars and their seasonal positions as viewed from earth.
The Zodiac: An imaginary belt in the heavens divided into twelve parts or
signs, each named for a different group of stars.

But since those twelve are quite well known,
she dreamed a pen to draw her own.

She'd draw an airplane on its way
to fly into the Milky Way,
then squint and draw a horse's head,
a stately cosmic thoroughbred.

Then she'd see a rocket ship
to take her on her deep space trip,
and marvel that these stars are suns
- even the faint and tiny ones.

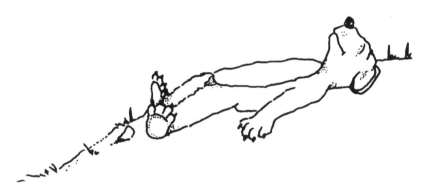

If all this sounds like fun to you,
perhaps someday you'll be there too,
deep in thought and observation
on the deck of a space station.

There you may find brand new stars,
two hundred times the size of ours,
or maybe help the world avoid
colliding with an asteroid.

So if you're captured by this thought...

...might YOU become an astronaut?

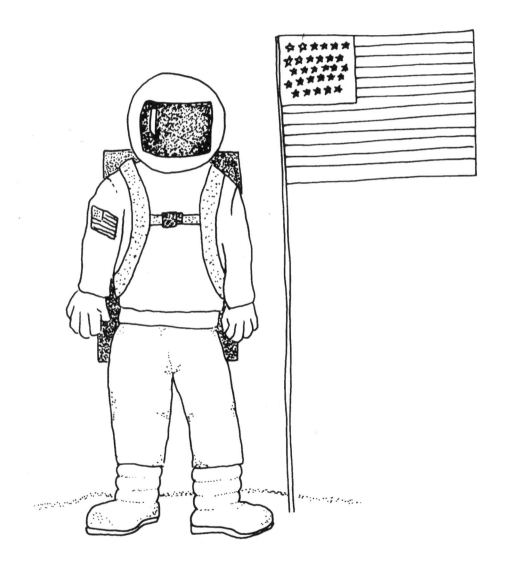

# WHEN EASTER EGGS HATCH

I dyed a crate of Easter Eggs,
pastels for the whole batch,
but I forgot to boil them first
so that they would not hatch.

Within four days I heard a chirp
from where the eggs were sitting.
I walked back to my Easter box,
one egg had started splitting.

A little feathered head poked out,
first two eyes then a beak...
but where the yellow tufts should be
there was a light blue streak!

The feathers were all purple,
pink, and different baby blues,
like there had been a spray paint fight
with paints of pastel hues.

Within a day there was a flock
of pastel colored chicks,
each color of the rainbow
in a bright and festive mix.

First there were a dozen,
but that dozen laid and hatched,
and soon there were two hundred,
with their colors all mismatched.

My house is now a chicken coop;
I live with non-stop crowing.
I kind of wish they'd run away,
but I don't think they're going!

So what to do with all of them?
Such birds you don't just eat.
Besides, I'd feel funny
serving pastel-colored meat.

So next year when I'm getting
my eggs ready to be dyed,
I'll break them in a frying pan
to first be poached and fried!

# FLYING NURSE

On nearly every summer night,
they make their rounds in silent flight.
But as you'll see, I'm quite averse
to getting "care" from such a nurse.

These small RNs of aviation,
flying in attack formation,
operate in cold collusion
to give me a blood transfusion.

And rather than a top med school,
they've trained inside a swampy pool,
which only fuels my grave frustration
with my unplanned blood donation.

Plus, I'm told, they're largely loath
to take the Hippocratic Oath,
in part because they DO do harm
when they are sucking on an arm.

Now if their training in the future
teaches them to stitch and suture,
maybe then I'll call them "nurses,"
but for now? ... they're flying curses.

---

RN: Registered Nurse
Collusion: Secret agreement.
Hippocratic Oath: An oath taken by doctors promising to practice
medicine ethically.

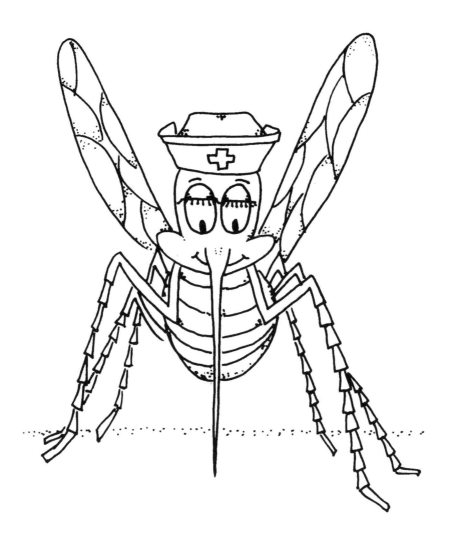

112

# BEYOND THE SEA

I'm not the first to wonder
what exists beyond the sea.
There is something in our nature
that is curious and free.

From Columbus to da Gama,
from Magellan to Cousteau,
they all wondered what's beyond the sea
until they had to know.

So last night instead of homework,
I watched hours of TV,
about sailing ships and pirates
who explored the world by sea.

But this morning I must wonder
if I should have got some rest,
perhaps done my composition,
maybe studied for my test?

'Cause I still am filled with wonder
at what is beyond the "C"...
as I stand to spell "chrysanthemum"
in this year's spelling bee!

## ALMOST

I almost grew an apple tree,
but forgot to plant the seed.
I planned to write a movie script
where I would play the lead.

I started to build a time machine,
to travel to the past.
I was going to lose at least five pounds,
but my diet didn't last.

I would have been a pilot,
if I liked to fly in planes.
I could have won a Nobel Prize,
if I had the brains.

I should have won a foot race,
if I'd run a faster mile.
I almost stopped to fold my clothes,
but they're still in a pile.

I nearly finished writing this poem, but...

## OUT HOUSE

I'm guessing that you've never seen
the bottom of a pit latrine.
But if you've looked down one you'll know
it's not a place you want to go.

That's why I'm making sure you're warned
about a creature, vile and horned,
who makes his house in such a pit
and pulls in people while they sit.

Beware that if he pulls you in,
you never will smell clean again!

The creature's called a "Bottom Biter."
He looks somewhat like a spider,
with suction cups instead of hands,
and legs that stretch like rubber bands.

The Bottom Biter has no nose,
which is a blessing, I'd suppose,
since with no nose he never thinks
that living in a toilet stinks.

Can you imagine being stuck
down in that pit with all that muck?

If you must go alone at night,
make sure you've got a megalite
to shine around inside that pit
before you even think to sit.

He's smaller than you might expect,
so you must carefully inspect
anywhere that he might hide
...which means you'll have to look inside.

He is a master of disguise,
but if a light's shined in his eyes
they will glow yellow like the sun...
if you see that, zip up and run!

## HALF A HOLE

Try to dig half a hole
next time you have a shovel.
Take whatever time you need
... I think you will have trouble.

# A PARTY FOR YOU, YOU AND YOU

I made a mistake while making a cake
and the cake rose amazingly high.
I'd increased the yeast so much that my feast
rose 'til it touched the sky.

This would not have been bad, except that I had
let my cat take a cat nap on top.
I thought it would rise, like most cakes or pies,
just a few inches then stop.

But it continued to rise, and to my surprise,
my cat and cake rose to the heavens.
I'm not a great cook, but it took just one look
to see just how well this yeast leavens.

I did not want to shake or knock over the cake
so the first thing that came to my mind,
was yell, "Come with a plate, this is gonna be great
and bring everyone you can find."

"It's a party for you, and your neighbors too,
and anyone you know who's nice.
Eat for Joe and then Jim, and then Faye after him,
'cause each birthday deserves a new slice."

And everyone everywhere wanted to come.
Soon other towns asked to come too.
And the local police said you must eat one piece
for every last person you knew.

All the singing, of course, soon made everyone hoarse,
and we burned every candle in town.
It took days to devour the eggs, milk and flour,
but together we got that cat down.

The cat met no harm and the local fat farm
did great business because of our feast.
We rescued the cat, we were happy and fat
and next time I'll measure the yeast.

120

# WILLIE POWER

Willie Watt was a powerful man,
but not like you might think.
A computer plugged into his brain
would whirl and flash and blink.

Even his hair was powerful,
standing straight on end,
like it was full of static,
black as coal and full of wind.

When power in the town went out
they turned to Willie Watt.
They tested him with jumper cables
and saw that he was "hot."

They rubbed a sock on Willie's head
to get the static flowing,
then fed him some plutonium
until he started glowing.

They knew they should have taken care
to ration Willie's force.
Instead they charged up everything
(short-sightedly, of course).

---

Plutonium: A radioactive element used in nuclear fission.

They each plugged in a TV set,
a washer and a fridge;
they lit the line of lights that lined
the lighthouse and the bridge.

They plugged in 14 other cords,
and now I must report,
when they plugged in the 15th cord
it caused his brain to short.

And though his brain was very strong,
the town's collective load
put Willie's brain on overload
and made his head explode!

The power this explosion took?
They say it's quite a lot.
The amount that killed ol' Willie
is now called a "Kilowatt."

## LOFT

I like my bed, it's really soft,
but since one's good, I built a loft.
I built them all up in a stack
for extra comfort for my back.

I bought two water beds on sale
and one air mattress, sent by mail.
Now I don't toss or turn or snore,
and I sleep great, I'm up to four!

Since four is good I will add others.
My fifth one was my baby brother's.
But I'm not done with adding on;
I bought a Japanese futon
that has a built in heated blanket.
When it's cold out I will thank it.

The bedding store that's in our mall
carries six brands; I bought them all.
One kind is made from high tech foam,
it's like a space lab in my home.

Now I've got twelve, I think I'll stop.
I hope that I can reach the top.
This bed is better, there is no doubt
... assuming that I don't fall out!

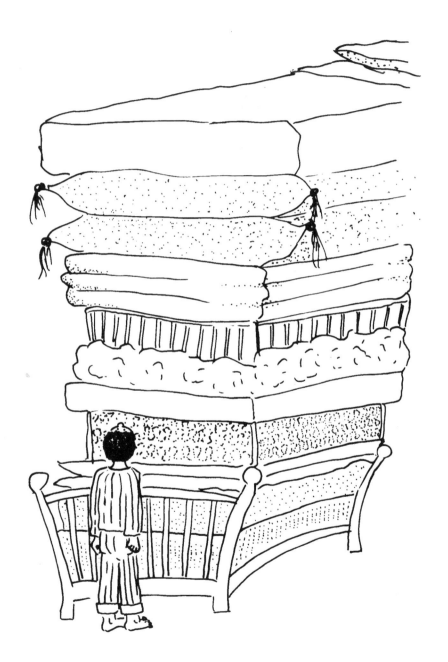

# DENTAL DELICACIES

Miss Foosa said, "I'm at a loss
why there is not more choice in floss,
that we can use to clean our gums
of gunk and plaque and gook and crumbs."

"I want some choices, plain or mint?
Why can't my dentist take a hint!
So I've designed a fresh replacement
in my lab down in the basement."

"Won't the users squeak and squeal
when floss tastes like a gourmet meal?
I'm sure they'd floss more than they do
if flossing tastes like Cordon Bleu."

"We'll also offer Key Lime Pie,
and sauerkraut on toasted rye.
And there's an after-dinner floss
that tastes like sweetened chocolate sauce."

"We're pretty sure it will sell out,
four million yards, or there about.
This concept's sure to be a hit,
so we will do much more with it."

"Now in my lab, under design,
I've got Ground Beef Straight-Tooth-Align.
Though while it's in, you should not eat,
your mouth will always taste like meat."

"We'll make your teeth both clean and straight
… just know your breath won't be that great."

# HUNGER STRIKE

I did not get a brand new bike,
so I went on a hunger strike.
I banged on buckets with my hands,
and read a list of my demands.

I shouted, "It is most unfair
that I am walking everywhere.
Bill and Bob got new beach cruisers.
They say walking is for losers."

"So 'til I get a brand new bike,
consider me on hunger strike!"

And just to make my strike complete,
I made a sign with "I won't eat."

I chanted chants and marched and howled,
and all the time my stomach growled.
My cries for justice were ignored.
I soon got hungry, tired and bored.

This hunger strike's a lousy deal.
I do not see the strike's appeal.
I still don't have a brand new bike,
and I can't eat the food I like!

## THE PILLOW CASE

Today I was searching the bedroom,
and though it sounds strange, it is true,
the cover that covers my pillow
has vanished with nary a clue!

My sheets are perfect and tidy.
My comforter's smooth as can be.
And yet, my pillow's uncovered
for all of the world to see.

I checked the floor, but no footprints.
The window was sealed up tight.
This one seemed like an inside job.
The pillow had put up no fight.

Under the bed were three boxes,
two books, and an old pair of shoes.
I found a blue ball I'd been missing,
but there were no pillow case clues.

I called in my terrier, Watson.
He quickly inspected the place.
Then Watson went digging for answers,
and searching for clues he could chase.

Frustrated, I soon lost interest.
I went out to watch some TV.
It seems that solving this pillow case
is more work than I thought it would be.

I later went looking for Watson.
On a pile of laundry he dozed.
Under his chin my pillow case sat.
Consider the pillow case closed.

## UP IN THE BASEMENT

An architect became renown
for building houses upside down,
and giving rooms peculiar placements
such as stairways up to basements.

Instead of A frames she made "V"s
with walls that sloped at odd degrees.
There is a couch, but you can't sit
unless you are strapped into it.

The whole thing was a puzzling sight.
The plumbing never did work right.
And every time that it would rain
the water would run up the drain.

# THE CAT ON THE KEYBOARD

I just returned to my keyboard
and sat down in my chair.
It seems that while I'd stepped away,
my cat had come through there.

He walked around the keyboard,
and I'm sorry to report,
that cat got me in trouble,
of an inconvenient sort.

I was drafting a short message
and got up to make a snack,
but my message had been sent for me
before I'd made it back.

I'd like to think that Susie
would have known that I spell better,
but that cat walked on my keyboard,
and typed Susie a love letter!

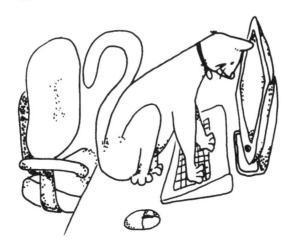

# ALTERNATIVE ENERGY

I do my part to help conserve.
I don't burn too much power.
I try not to be wasteful
and I don't sing in the shower.

So when I saw a sign that read
"New Free-Range Energy,"
I knew that this was something
that I simply had to see.

I knew I must investigate,
so I went to that store
and the owner called right out to me
as I walked in the door.

"I've got a flock of lightning bugs
inside my jacket pocket.
You never need to plug them in,
or charge them in a socket.

You keep them on your person,
and whenever you need light,
you open up your pocket
and you let the bugs take flight!"

My disbelief was evident
and I was on the fence.
And so he tried to draw me in,
in hopes he could convince

me to simply try them out,
to take a test set home,
and place them right beside my bed,
inside a crystal dome.

But I'd need ten in every room,
my needs were quite extensive,
and as we talked it through it seemed,
the price was too expensive.

I told him this and thanked him
and I turned to walk away,
but before I could get out the door
he tempted me to stay.

"Before you go, make sure you know,
there's lots of other lighting.
I've got a pheasant that's phosphorescent,
now isn't THAT exciting?"

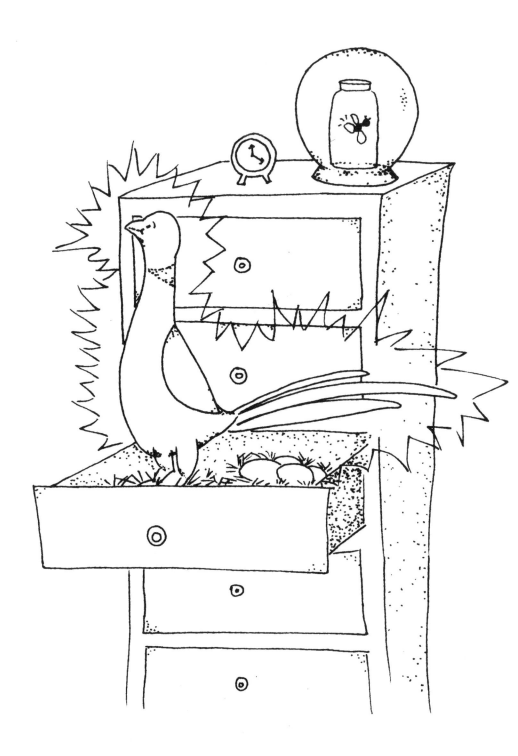

I will say I was quite impressed
to see that glowing bird,
but birds make lots of noise at night –
at least that's what I've heard.

She'd probably nest inside my drawer,
and lay eggs in my pants.
I know it might not happen,
but I'd hate to take the chance.

'Cause if she hatched her brood at home,
and they lived in my closet,
they'd make the place shine oh so bright,
that they'd likely cause it

to be impossible to sleep,
or study for my classes.
Why just to walk into the room,
I'd have to wear sunglasses!

And I know birds can make a stink
(I've seen a chicken coop)
- especially when there's lots of them
all nesting in a group.

So I said, "Thanks, I'm quite impressed,
her plumage does glow bright –
but could you show me something else?
The pheasant's not quite right."

He said, "Of course, why - silly me!
Let's look at something cleaner,
and birds can grow so big and wide,
I'll show you something leaner."

"I'll show you something stronger,
something with a tad more juice;
I'll make you a deal on an electric eel,
he's perfect for home heating use."

"The Navy's using eel power
aboard their newest ships.
It only takes one eel to make
two round the world trips."

"Make no mistake about it,
he has got a lot of volts.
He's sizzling with more current
than the brightest lightning bolts."

It seemed like I could save some cash,
and cut my power bill.
So I said, "Sure, I'll take him,
why, yes-siree I will."

And I drove home then, feeling good
about what I had spent;
I'd save both my electric bill
and the environment.

I should have bought instructions,
they were $14.92,
but he made it sound so easy,
I'd just figure what to do.

I put him in the bathtub
with my TV and hair dryer,
and sure enough, there was a spark!
... but then there was a fire.

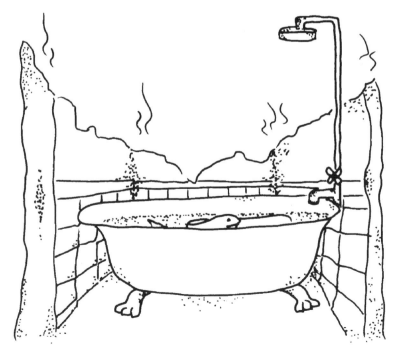

# THE NATURE POLICE

Some frogs have jobs
and so do some geese.
And me? I'm a robin,
and Chief of Police.
I'm enforcing the rules
and keeping the peace.
And that's how I spend my day.

I check the road runner
to make sure he's not speeding.
I make sure the raccoon
paid for what he is eating.
I respond when the sheep
in the meadow are bleating.
And that's how I spend my day.

If a goose has got loose
and fowl play is suspected...
since the condor's endangered
he must be protected.
If the possum plays dead
the crime scene is inspected.
And that's how I spend my day.

I'll ticket a cricket
for chirping too loudly.
I'll make way for ducklings
who're walking through proudly.
I'll subpoena a weasel
who's lying avowedly.
And that's how I spend my day.

As nature's police
my work's never quite done;
so I don't get much rest.
I don't get thanked a ton.
I keep the animals safe
so they can have fun.
And that's how I spend my day.

---

Subpoena: A written order demanding that a person come to a court of law.
Avowedly: Openly, knowingly.

# DRUM SET

My drum set has a lot of drums
that I must always bring,
with microphones and drum sticks
and my drummer benchy thing.

But I'm spacey and forgetful
and at one big show last summer,
I forgot one drum at home,
which was a major bummer.

I did not forget a bass drum,
nor a symbol, nor a snare...
I forgot my ear drum
and nobody had a spare!

## SHADOW OF A DOUBT

For years Joe had been free to roam,
in peace, at night, throughout the home,
to scrounge for scraps of old Swiss cheese,
or do whatever he might please -
just one of many mice inside,
that ate and squeaked and multiplied
until the growing population
had become an infestation.

When mouse droppings were everywhere
Mrs. Branner shouted, "I declare
I will not live with all these mice,
and do not make me tell you twice!"
And so, to put an end to that,
Mr. Branner bought a cat.
He turned the big cat loose inside,
which made the mouse tribe mortified.

At 3AM, two nights ago,
this quiet mouse, our hero, Joe,
looked out the window, at the night,
completely awestruck by the light
reflected from the moon and snow,
that made the kitchen window glow
an eerie sort of yellow green,
a color Joe had never seen.

From high up on that window sill,
Joe watched the snow fall, quiet and still.
And when he finally turned around,
Joe saw his shadow on the ground.
Because the house was dark inside,
the glowing moonlight did provide
long shadow light upon the wall,
which made Joe's shadow two feet tall.

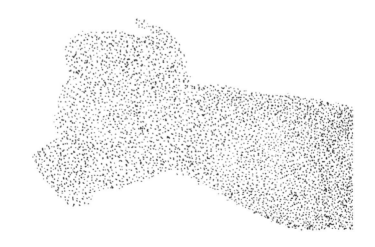

Joe swelled with pride, "I've grown so large that I should be the mouse in charge."

Some other mice Joe kinda knew
had also seen Joe's shadow too,
and these mice nearly popped their eyes
at how much Joe had grown in size.

They said, "If you've grown as strong as that,
you ought to drive away the cat!
And if you do, then our belief
is that you should become our chief."

Their praise continued, Joe grew proud.
He started squeaking high and loud
about his strength and his routine
to take down any cat they'd seen.

Within two minutes, word had spread
that Joe would strike the big cat dead.
They showered him with heaps of praise;
then they suggested lots of ways
that the big cat could be dispatched,
and then, for Joe, a plan was hatched.

They woke the cat up as they'd planned.
Joe bravely squeaked, "I understand
that you are looking for a meal,
so I will offer you a deal.
Right now we fight, with teeth and claws.
It's no holds barred, the only law's
that if you lose you'll leave this house.
But win? Eat me, a twelve pound mouse."

With that he stretched tall as he could,
convinced that his great mouse size would
prompt the cat to run away,
and he'd be chief by break of day.

Instead, the cat just laughed out loud,
"You're as ignorant as you are proud!"

The cat took Joe with little fight,
and Joe's last thought was, "Serves me right.
The ardent praise I came to cherish
is the reason I will perish.
Pride made my thinking quite unclear,
they told me what I'd want to hear.
I thought that I'd be chief of mice,
instead I'll be a sacrifice."

The moral, as you've probably guessed
is, "Never become too impressed
with praise that others heap on you
...especially if it's not true!"

## TOSSED SALAD

My dear Aunt Bea said, "Please help me!
I'm kind of in a crunch.
Just 90 minutes from right now
The Queen will come for lunch."

"She didn't give much notice,
so I only just now knew
that The Royal Queen of England
will be shortly passing through."

"And further, when the messenger
arrived with his report,
he said we must prepare a lunch
for her entire court!"

Bea tasked me with a salad,
then she ran off to get dressed,
in her finest gown and earrings
so The Queen would be impressed.

Salad for two hundred?
What a monumental task.
I didn't know what I should do,
or whom that I could ask.

I didn't have much time to spare.
I'd have to improvise.
How could I wash and gather
all the fixin's and supplies?

She'd said to throw in anything
that's leafy, fresh and green.
But that would overflow the sink,
and so... the washing machine!

It seemed like an ingenious plan
to wash off all the dirt;
and if I did not add the soap,
it surely couldn't hurt.

I put in twenty lettuce heads,
some iceberg and endive,
and stripped some leaves from household plants
that looked to be alive.

Next up, I added apples,
and two heaping walnut sacks.
Then I threw in cranberries,
in four dozen large-sized packs.

I dumped some salad dressing
in the fabric softener tray,
then set it for a soft wash,
closed the door, and walked away.

When I thought about the tossing,
and the steps it would require,
it seemed the perfect shortcut
was to toss it in the dryer.

When the wash cycle had ended,
right after the final spin,
I opened up the dryer door
and stuffed the washed greens in.

I added croutons and sharp knives;
the machine would do the rest.
I thought, "In 60 minutes
it will all be tossed and dressed."

Two minutes 'fore the cycle's end
The Queen entered the room,
but the dryer stole her thunder
with a thunderous loud "Boom!"

The dryer had exploded,
dressing in the pipes I'd guess,
and the fiery leaf explosion
made The Queen a royal mess!

This explosion is the reason
why you'll never find today,
a restaurant in all of England
that will serve Salad Flambée.

## MOON VIEW

I dreamed I woke up on the moon;
I can't remember why.
I noticed when you're on the moon,
the moon's not in the sky.

It was peaceful looking back at earth,
glowing blue and green and bright.
It's beautiful here on the moon;
the earth is full tonight.

Next stop:

Wherever your imagination takes you!

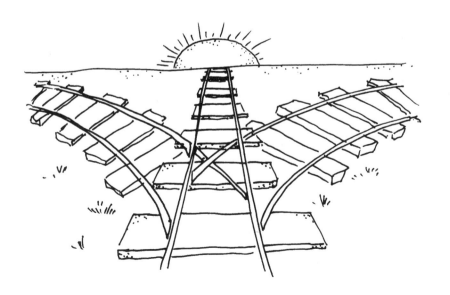

# ACKNOWLEDGMENTS

Hans would like to thank Mimi and Poppy Lemur for their tireless support and for instilling a love of language and wordplay at an early age. Hans and Jen would both like to thank Mimi Lemur for her eagle-eyed editorial acumen and her constructive critiques. Jen would like to thank her parents, grandma and grandpa Foosa for many things, but mostly for their love and support, which have allowed her to try new things. She would also like to thank Nana Test for sharing her love of art and creativity.

We have received a tremendous amount of support in this process from friends and family, and while the list is too long to recount here in its entirety, please know that your contributions are appreciated! In particular, we would like to thank the troop of six to twelve year olds who reviewed various drafts of the book and shared their literary expertise. Thank you to you and your parents for being honored members of Team Lemur!

Big thanks also to the following: Kimberly Schwede for her design and creation of a fantastic cover...Richard Gorsuch for sharing his vast book design expertise... Stanford English professor Ken Fields for his feedback and suggestions... the Wente family for encouraging people to push their creative limits... the El Dorado crew for keeping story-telling alive...Haley Bird and Parker Dog for numerous things (big and little) throughout the process... the lemurs of Madagascar for inspiring us with their friendly, curious and social personalities... and the family, teachers, coaches, friends and travel partners who have supported and inspired us in the great adventure of life. This collection would not be possible without you!

## ABOUT THE AUTHORS

Hans and Jen attribute much of their interest in education to their mothers, who are both retired school teachers. Jen earned a bachelor's degree in Sociology and a master's degree in Education from Stanford University. Hans holds a bachelor's degree in Economics from Stanford and an M.B.A. from The University of Pennsylvania's Wharton School.

Hans and Jen's love of reading was honed at an early age through the works of writers like Dr. Seuss and Shel Silverstein. They hope that Mister Lemur may inspire others to read, write and dream.

The most important book review,
is the one that's done by you.
So open the pages and read a few,
and then decide what you'd like to do.